Poetic IMAGERY

Ellen Summers

NEWMAN SPRINGS PUBLISHING
320 Broad Street
Red Bank, NJ 07701

First originally published by Newman
Springs Publishing 2022

ISBN 979-8-88763-049-6 (Paperback)
ISBN 979-8-88763-050-2 (Digital)

Printed in the United States of America

I would like to dedicate this book to all those
who allowed me to include their names, and
those who cheered me on, alive and deceased.

Contents

Acknowledgments

I would like to express my gratitude to everyone who helped make this book possible.

This book is in memory of those mentioned here who are no longer with us.

Gratitude to those who are named in here that have brought inspiration and those who have believed in me.

Introductions

Self-Introduction

My name
Is Ali
I'm a poet
And I know it
Have something
To show
For it
Easily influenced
By people, places
And things
Especially the weather
Pen and paper
Do the talking
Like a brush
On an easel
Imaginable scenery
Is my thing
I want you
To see
What I see
In my mind
While writing
These poems

I Am Me

I am someone
Who has a heart
Good intentions
Priorities and goals
Don't be shy
Be confident
In yourself
What I do
Is my concern
Nobody else's
I'm doing
What's best
For me
I am
An introvert
That should
Speak up
And be heard
Past
Doesn't matter
The present moment
Counts
Family comes first
You know
Who your
True friends are
Who am I?
I am me

Memorial Poems

Grandma Memories

Oh, the memories
Weekends in Garden City
Spent with Grandma
Old country songs
From her vast collection
Playing on arrival
Evenings at Herbie's
Buggy rides
Those were the times
Down the street
To Dewey's house
Sleeping on the couch
Or on a cot
Waking up on Sundays
Breakfasts with bacon
The drives there
Were a bit long
But worth it
Trips to Harrisonville
Down the winding
Back road
Seeing movies
Or going swimming
Walks around
The quiet block
Following the uneven sidewalk
Life was good
While at Grandma's

Up she goes
To go see Art
At the old cedar
In the sky
To sit beside
One another
Holding hands
In a booth
Catching up
On missed memories
Coffee and conversation
She is missed
Her laugh
Still echoes
In my mind
Wonderful memories
Surface
Grandmas
Are like
Antique little girls
Who will leave
Lipstick smudges
On your face
Lasting impressions
In your heart

Memories of Grandma

My grandma
A sweet lady
She is missed
The joy
In her voice
When she
Ran into
Someone familiar
At the store
I see her
Up there
Sitting with art
Holding hands
On a porch swing
Reminiscing
Of years past
As we gather
From time to time
She remains
A fond memory
To be treasured
Grandma,
Tell me about
The good ol' days

In Loving Memory of
Herbie Baumhoff

Buggy rides
Road trips
Family gatherings
Always
Had a drink
In his hand
Stories
To tell
Vehicles
To work on
Hugs
To give
His voice
Still echoes
In my mind
He's not hurting
Anymore
He is missed
Already

In Loving Memory of Lindsey Brown

Lindsey
Taken too soon
A bright light
For many
Her smile
Known by many
Best hugs
At the reunions
So much
In store
Cut short
All we ask
Lindsey
Say hi
To Alice
And Reenie
For us
Send them
Our love
Why did
You have
To leave
So Soon?

Uncle Sid
Up you went
To reunite
With Janice
Your brothers
And sisters
Greeting you
With open arms
Welcome home
They declare
As you enter
Through the front gate
No longer in pain
Breathing easier
As he is
Catching up
And exchanging memories
Bottles of beer
With fishing poles
And tackle boxes
Card games
And cigarettes
You caught one
Reel it in
Janice close by

Making some jewelry
You are missed
And most certainly
Loved

In Loving Memory of Ronald Pracht

Ruth and family
All of you
Have been on
My mind lately
It's beyond
Difficult
Seeing someone
Go through
This much pain
Right now
I wish for you
Love, comfort,
Peace
And let's not forget
Lots of hugs
Let the memories
Come from all
Directions
Ron and his Braum's
Indulgences
Ornery nature
Working in the yard
Or kicking back

To watch a movie
Sending love
And hugs
From Texas

Poems for People

For Jay Collins

Long walks
Downtown
"Gimme your hand"
Strolls around the jail
We did prevail
Get back
Tippy cat
Weekly visits
Miss those
Getting to the intercom
Talking in Spanish
Wisecrack remarks
Made in return
We go back
Down on Vail
Keeps things interesting
With his
Joking nature
Wishing you the best
For your progress
And safety
Remain peaceful
Keep your head up
The impossible
Is possible
Keep on
Flying
Jaybird

For Amelia Varner

Back in the day
We wanted
To be
Invisible
Locations and time
Separated us
We began again
Right where
We left off
Trips to KC
Artsy time
Painting, pottery
We could speak
Gibberish like minions
And get what
We're trying to say
Through thick and thin
Good times and bad times
You are my bestie
When we are old
And wrinkly
Look back
And laugh
At how silly
We were
When we
Were just whippersnappers

Old Friend

She awoke from the haze
Gathering herself
Saw someone in the distance
He stepped toward her
And hugged her
As if she was an old friend
He hadn't seen
In a while
They both smiled
In the silliest way
She couldn't help but think
Hadn't seen him before
Looking into his eyes
A relief came over her
That she hadn't felt before
She felt welcomed
And loved
For who she is
No matter her flaws
For the first time
In a while
She's glad to say
Feels respected
And that she is important
To someone
His arms
Every time
Her favorite place to be

Nature Poems

Autumn

Leaves
Falling off
The trees
Like rain
Acorns
Scattered on the sidewalk
Be careful
Not to slip
And slide
Like a cartoon character
Falling
On your butt
Mild October
Beautiful colors
Go find
A pile of leaves
Jump in it
Pretend you're swimming
Enjoy this time
It won't be here
For long
Cold temps
Will send you
Jumping
Into blankets

Camping with Friends

Feet on the dash
In the truck
Off to play
In the water
Leave the week's
Issues behind
Enjoy the scenery
No worries
No problem
Come back
Sun-kissed
Clear minded
Relaxed
Sitting by
The fire
Watching
The wood burn
Hearing the flames
Crackle
Spending time
With good friends
Memories
To be had
Laughs to ensue
Shenanigans
To follow

Cornfields Forever

Miles from civilization
Vast fields
Farms galore
Corn silos
Circle drive
Cows roaming
In stripped fields
Nebraska skies
Roads leading
Through the middle
Of nowhere
Mixtures of cars
And farm equipment
Decorate the
Countryside
All you hear
In the quiet night
Are vehicles
Headed down
An open road
Flatlands here
Hills and valleys there
If the stars are out
Grab a lawn chair
And a drink
Here's to peace and quiet

Floral Admiration

Tulips
To the right
Roses
To the left
Daisies
In front of you
Petunias
Off to the side
Flowers
All around
A beautiful sight
Take it in
Snap a photo
Soak it up
Wind chimes
Playing a symphony
In the breeze
A wooden bench
Amongst
The flowers
To pause
Floral beauty
To be adored
Make a bouquet
Give it to
Someone you love
Today

Fly Away

Sometimes
I wish
I could
Take off
Like a bird
Run like the wind
Spread my wings
And fly away
Out into
The open sky
Without a care
In the world
Drifting through the clouds
Nothing holding me down
Greeting birds
Passing by
No track of time
Up high
In the sky
Clear mind
Heart
Full of peace

Fort Snow

Pow!
In the face
With a snowball
You've been hit
Brush off
That ammo
Time
For payback
Avoid yellow snow
Build a fort
Go into hiding
And start
A snowball war
Remember
To go inside
Once in a while
Or you
Will freeze
Your butt off
Homemade chicken noodle soup
Or even hot cocoa
Will warm you
Right up
To bundle back up
Outside we go
Snowballs and forts
Galore

Frosty Memories

Blades of grass
Protruding
From the
Pristine white
Sparkling snow
Slippery roads
And sidewalks
Sun is out
Snowmen
And snow angels
To be made
Rosy cheeks
Wet boots
Smiling faces
Don't forget
To go sledding
With dear friends
Then warm up
With hot beverages
Or soup
Some of the
Best memories
Come from
A winter wonderland

In the Country

Down in the boonies
No phone service
Off the beaten path
Away from everything
The way it should be
Yard art galore
Street signs
Nowhere to be found
Windows open
Breeze through the trees
Nothing but the sounds
Of the surroundings
To take your mind away
From the day's headaches
Fishing poles
And tackle boxes
Sandals
And lawn chairs
Look at that
You caught something
Reel it in
And hold it up
For anyone to see
Put it back
These are the days
Soak up the rays

Joys of the Seasons

Beyond those trees
Pond to the side
Winding gravel driveway
To a quiet place
Relax
Let fun be had
Cherished life
Away from
The hustle and bustle
Of the busy city
Winter nights
By the fire
Hot beverages
And warm pajamas
Memories
Of years past
Summers spent
Roaming about
Barefoot
In tank tops
And shorts
Life is short
Savoring every moment
Until life's
Joys begin

Let It Rain

Don't be afraid
To get soaked
By the rain
You might
Feel better afterwards
Whatever is bothering you
Let it rinse
That rain
Can wash away
More than you know
Mind body and soul
Dark clouds
Rain sounds
On the roof
And the ground
Puddles to be found
Feet
To get dirty
Mud fights
May happen
Muddy footprints
To trail
Through the house

Nebraska

New scenery
Different skies
Windmill neighborhood
Four-wheeler tracks
Across the mud
Boot prints
Through the gravel
Smell of brush fires
Faint in the air
Where are you?
Smack-dab
In farm country
Nebraska
Don't know
Much of it
Passed through
Many years ago
Lots of
Small rural towns
Semitrucks flood
I-80
Truck stops
Line the roadway
Feel free
To pass
That combine
Slowing you down

Peace

Wind through
Long wavy
Locks
Grabby toes
Gripping
The green grass
Sunshine upon
My face
Sounds of
Cicadas and crickets
In the
Background
Wide-open
Spaces
Call your
Name
Quiet enough
To hear
Yourself
Think
A melody
From some
Nearby
Wind chimes
Sun tea
On the porch
Take it
All in
And be
At peace

Through the Clouds

Here I am
Flying high
Admiring
My surroundings
At a
Cruising altitude
Looking ahead
Smile on my face
Getting things done
Hope to succeed
Try not
To get distracted
And fly
Into a tree
You can do this
Are much capable
Pay no attention
To naysayers
Prove them wrong
Show them
You are strong

Time with Nature

Nothing more beautiful
Than a patriotic sky
Fireflies
Light up the night
Guide you
Through the wilderness
Bugbites indicate
You had some nature time
Not to be disturbed
By work or home
Frogs, crickets, and cicadas
Provide the only sounds
To be around
Forget what's bothering you
Get lost in the scene
Let your mind wander
Leave the past behind
It is time
For you
To unwind
And be kind
To your mind
Take a seat
Prop your feet
Make a drink

Winter

Sound of snow
Beneath your feet
How neat
Snow angels
In the distance
Try to catch
A snowflake
Go skate
On an icy lake
But don't fall through
Whatever you do
Are your
Fingers and toes
numb yet?
Sledding
Brings back
Memories
The steeper
The hill
The faster you go
Whoa!
What a way
To go!

Inspirational Poems

A New Day

Sunshine
Leaves on the ground
Jackets in the morning
It's a new day
New challenges
Things to do
People to see
Leave the past days
Worries behind
Take on new opportunities
Enjoy the present
Appreciate those
Who are there
For you
Don't forget
You must
Be there
For them too
Remember to breathe
When things get tough
Find your nearest relative
Or even friend
Give them a hug
Be their cheerleader
Everyone
Needs a little
Encouragement

Beach Therapy

As the waves
Crash
Against my legs
Negative energy
Leaves me
And washes away
With the tide
Leaving footprints
In the sand
Picking up seashells
Admiring the scenery
Of the beach
Taking in
The sounds
Digging my feet
Into the sand
Feeling
The primitive energies
Breaking free
From the sand
With
A fresh perspective

Clarity

Everything
Couldn't be any clearer
You know what
You want
Can get there
Discouragement
Is the enemy
Knew it was time
For new scenery
Will you come back?
You're not sure yet
Other places
Are on your mind
Nobody
Can hold you back now
In charge
Of your own destiny
Be yourself
Hang on to those
Who encourage
Your self-expression
Leave behind
That cruel summer
And the baggage
Deceitful
Disappointing, hateful people
Embrace the needed growth
Back to normal

Determination

A few potholes
One dead-end sign
Change that tire
Keep on going
Take the trail
Avoid the nails
And the screws
Look to that horizon
For something new
Don't let that cloud of smoke
Lead you astray
Push through it
You will see those
Who truly care
Right there
Ready to see you
Wondering how you have been
Willing to talk
You have missed them
Don't forget
About your cheerleaders
Forget the haters
Pay no attention
To the clowns
Trying to trip you
Let them fall
All by themselves

Earthling

Step out
Into the sunshine
Close your eyes
Take in
The welcome warmth
Breathe in
Good vibes
Exhale
The negative
Look to
The sky
Get lost
In the clouds
Go barefoot
In the green grass
Earth
Between your toes
Feel the energy
Protons
And electrons
Go ahead
Prance
Through your yard
I won't tell
Anyone

For the Birds

Here comes
A bluebird
Looking for seed
Cardinals
Jumping
With glee
Meadowlarks
In the park
Robins
Bobbin
On the branches
Hummingbirds
And their wings
Fluttering
At full speed
Oh look!
A dove
Is it in love?
Look out
Below!
Bird poop

Mindful Thinking

Breathe in
And out
Take it easy
Think
Very carefully
What's going
Through your head
Is it within
Your control
Past is in the past
The future
Isn't here yet
Stay present
You are needed
Right here
And now
Don't let
That hurtful thought
Drown you out
You are okay
Living and breathing
Rise above this
And continue
To shine

Monday Inspiration

Back to work
Or school
We all know
The weekend
Went too fast
Don't let
It be
A manic Monday
Instead
Welcome
A new week
With new
Challenges ahead
Keep those
Monday blues
Away
Raise that
Hot beverage mug
Cheers!
Here's to
Monday!

Perseverance

Looking to the sky
Tunes in my ears
Getting lost in the stars
Can't help but wonder
What's next for me
I finally did it
Got that degree
Associates isn't much
But it's something
Took me long enough
Now what
A few things linger
Not sure
What to reach for
Looking for something
To support myself
I shouldn't let stipulations
Stop me
From moving forward
Medical field is a given
There are many people
Out there
Who are just starting out
It's never too late to start
Don't let those further along
Discourage your progress
Listen to that baseline
Get lost in it

You know what
You want to do
It will come
To you

Smile Lines

Two hands
Clasped together
Holding on
To one another
Smiles across
Aged faces
You can tell
Their love
Has withstood
The test of time
By their
Body language
Very welcoming
To see
Elderly couples
With that spark
That tends to fade
As time goes on
Lasting marriage
They can't
Go anywhere
Without
Their soulmate

Step Back

It's a bad day
But you know what
You can rise above this
Remember
What you
Already have
And feel grateful
Today
Is just today
Tomorrow
Is another opportunity
To be great
Improvements
Are possible
Leave yesterday
Behind
Be present
In right now
And know that
Everything
Is going
To be okay

Speak Up!

Nobody is perfect
Everyone has faults
Accept
And move forward
Speak up
And be heard
Try not to hide
And become
Unheard of
How will
Someone know
If something
Is wrong
When nothing
Is said
Not everybody
Can read
Your mind
Please
Be kind
To yourself
We all know
We're our own
Worst enemy

True Story

Karma
Everyone has it
Expected or unexpected
Humbling
Or life lesson
Be mindful
Of how
You treat
Others
That mistreatment
Will find you
And pay
It forward
We are
All the same
Pride and prejudice
Discrimination and hatred
Is not needed
Don't be mean
Then demand
Respect in return
Things don't
Work that way

Words to Live By

One life
Live it
One day
At a time
Communicate
With integrity
Care with
Compassion
Be understanding
During tough times
Give
Your undivided attention
Take pride
In the simple things
Give hugs
When they are wanted
And needed
Apologize
After wrongdoing
Complications
Are inevitable
Stand up straight
Respond when
Spoken to
Leave the past
In the past
Wait patiently

For the future
Live for
Right now
In the present

Silly Poems

A Cat's Life

Easy
With those claws
I'm not
Your scratching post
Go pick on
The dog
Quit eating grass
I don't want
To find an "eww!"
In my shoe
A litter track
On my bed
You little turkey
What's this?
Cat hair
In my food
Yuck!
Furry monster
Why must you
Leave surprises
For me to step in
Then turn around
And purr in my lap?

A Dog's Life

That nose
Is cold!
There's that
Wagging tail
Dog hair
Everywhere
Don't sniff that!
Get away from there
I know that look
You chewed my book
Crook!
Pieces
Of dog food
Trail through
The kitchen
Toys
In the hallway
Muddy paw prints
Trail through
The house
Slobber
On your
Pant leg

Bathe, Escape

Ten monkey toes
Protruding
From the water
Are your fingers
Wrinkly yet?
Soak a little longer
Let your worries
Float away
Then go down
The drain
Don't slip
And slide
On your way
Out
Emerge from
That tub
Relaxed
And renewed
Then shout
"How do you like me now?!"

Shenanigans

Sliding down
The hallway
In your socks
And underpants
Silly chants
Echo
Off the walls
The dog
Glaring at you
Then gets out
Of the way
Cat doesn't care
Thinks you're square
But you
Don't have a care
They don't dare
Disturb you
In la-la land
Tea is ready
Go get dressed
Work awaits
Don't let
Anything
Break your stride

Space Cadet

Yes
I caught you
Staring into space
The lights are on
But nobody
Is home
What's inside
Of that mind
Of yours
Earth to you
Talk to me
Come back down
Or I will
Poke you
With a ten-foot pole
Until you answer me
Don't give me
That look
Guilty
It's written
All over
Your face

Closing

<hr>

I hope you have enjoyed these poems and was able to picture some of them in your mind. New ones are always being written. Memories and peace are my intention.